Voices of the Heart

ED YOUNG

Scholastic Press / New York

Published by Scholastic Press, a division of Scholastic Inc., *Publishers since 1920.*

No part of this publication may be reproduced in whole or in part, or stored in a retrieval
system, or transmitted in any form or by any means, electronic, mechanical, photocopying,
recording, or otherwise, without written permission of the publisher. For information regarding
permission, write to Scholastic Press, 555 Broadway, New York, NY 10012.

Library of Congress Cataloging-in-Publication Data
Young, Ed.
Voices of the heart /by Ed Young.   p. cm.
ISBN 0-590-50199-2
1.Emotions. 2.Virtues. I.Title.
BF511.Y68 1997
179'.9—dc20   96-7595

12 11 10 9 8 7 6 5 4 3 2 1   7 8 9/9 0 1 2/0
Printed in the U.S.A.   36
First printing, March 1997

Calligraphy for the jacket and title page is by John Stevens.
The text of this book is set in Adobe Garamond.
The author/illustrator used a variety of materials in his mixed-media collages,
including handmade and hand-dyed papers.

To Professor M. C. Cheng who guided me

back to the riches of our own heritage.

Voices
of the Heart

Virtue
The heart is good.

惠　De

Shame
The heart knows right from wrong.

恥　Chi

Realization
The heart reaches complete understanding.

悟　Wu

Forgiveness
The heart accepts everything.

恕　Shu

Joy
A happy heart.

悦　Yueh

Sorrow
A sad heart.

悲　Bei

Respect
The heart honors others.

恭　Gong

Rudeness
The heart is disrespectful.

慢　Man

Contentment
A peaceful heart.

慸　Ying

Despair
An anxious heart.

急　Qi

Laziness
An idle heart.

惰　Duo

Ability
A strong heart.

態　Tai

Grace
The heart shows pity.

恩　En

Forgetfulness The heart loses its sense of purpose.		忘	Wang
Resentment The heart is bitter.		怨	Yan
Constancy The heart is faithful.		恆	Heng
Aspiration The heart has goals.		志	Chi
Panic A frightened heart.		慌	Huang
Mercy A compassionate heart.		慈	Tsi
Worry A fearful heart.		愁	Chou
Patience The heart grows tolerant.		忍	Ren
Wrath An angry heart.		忿	Feng
Stifled A silenced heart.		悶	Men
Evil The heart cannot express its goodness.		惡	Ao
Doubt The heart stops trusting.		惑	Huo
Loyalty The heart is certain.		忠	Zhong

Virtue

The heart is good.

+ ten

田 eyes

匚 right angle, meaning rightness

When ten pairs of eyes see and agree on something, it is considered right or straight. When others acknowledge straightness in a person, he is considered upright. Virtue is the straightness of the heart.

Shame

The heart knows
right from wrong.

 ear

 Put your ears to your heart.
A person who knows right
from wrong has a sense of
shame.

Realization

The heart reaches complete understanding.

 five senses, symbolizing all things and completion

 mouth

 The number "five" represents the five senses, five elements, five colors, five tastes, and five systems of the body. When the heart is in harmony with the five senses, it is aware. This leads to realization.

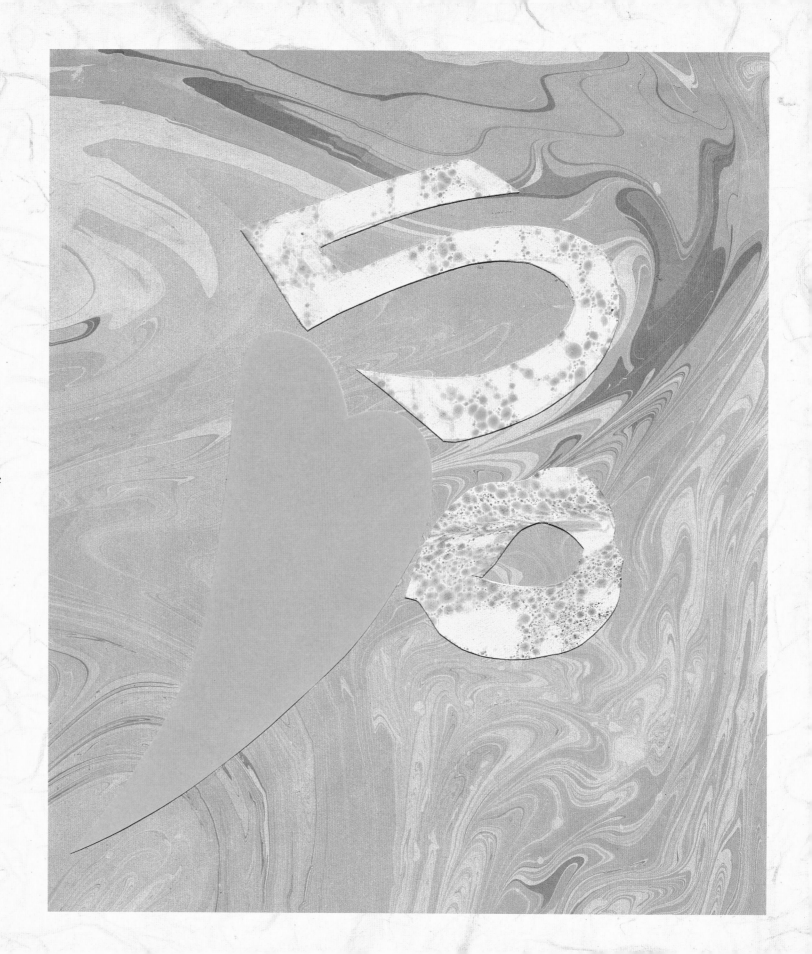

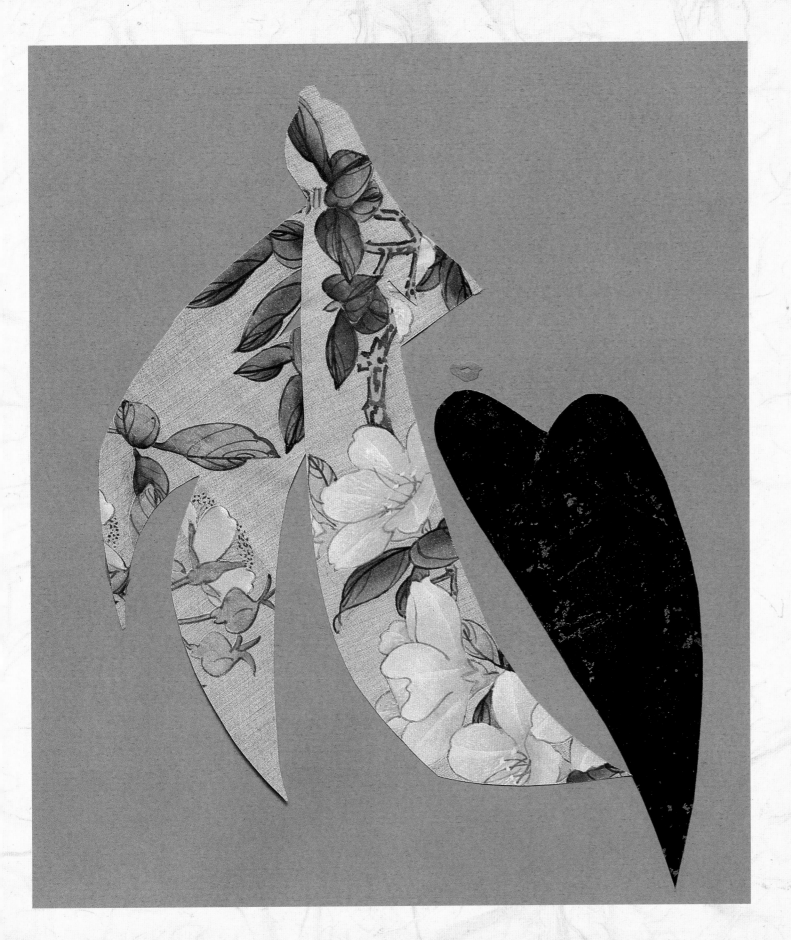

Forgiveness

The heart accepts
everything.

 woman, symbolizing empathy,
sharing feeling with others

 mouth

 The heart forgives when it
accepts and acknowledges
conflict without blame.

Joy

A happy heart.

 words

 mouth

 two legs

The mouth and legs together represent an older person. Wise words from a respected person bring good fortune and joy to the heart.

Sorrow

A sad heart.

 opposites

Sorrow arises when the heart
is ruled by feelings that
oppose each other.

Respect

The heart honors others.

 twenty

 pairs of hands

Twenty pairs of hands symbolize twenty generations. When the heart acknowledges the wisdom of twenty generations, respect develops.

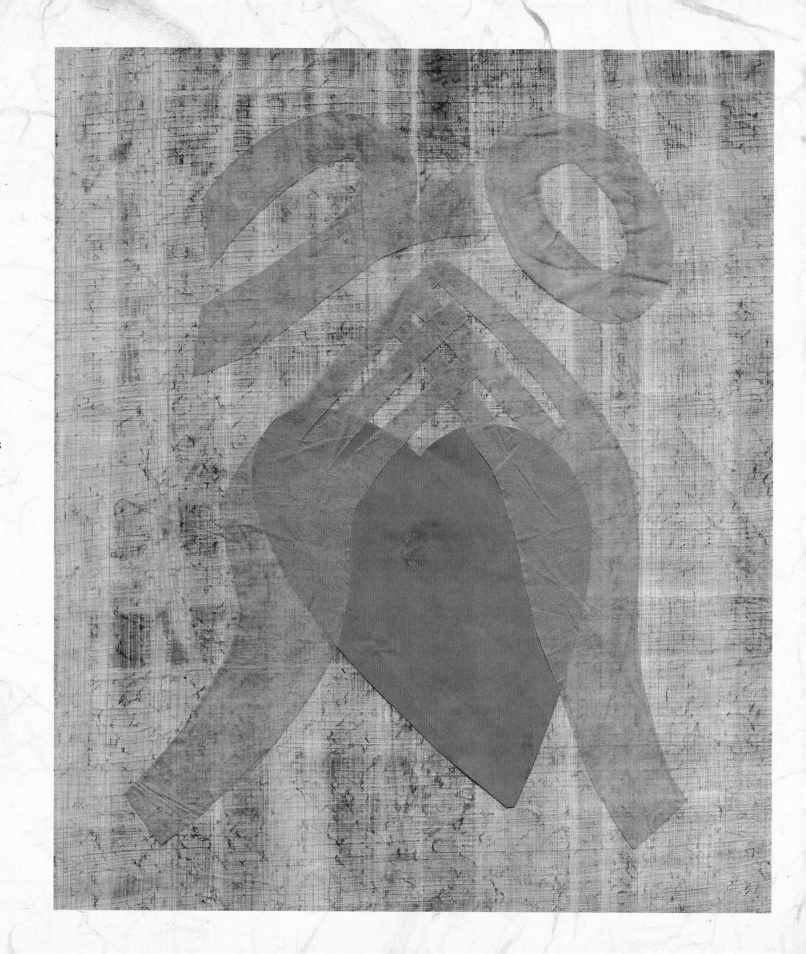

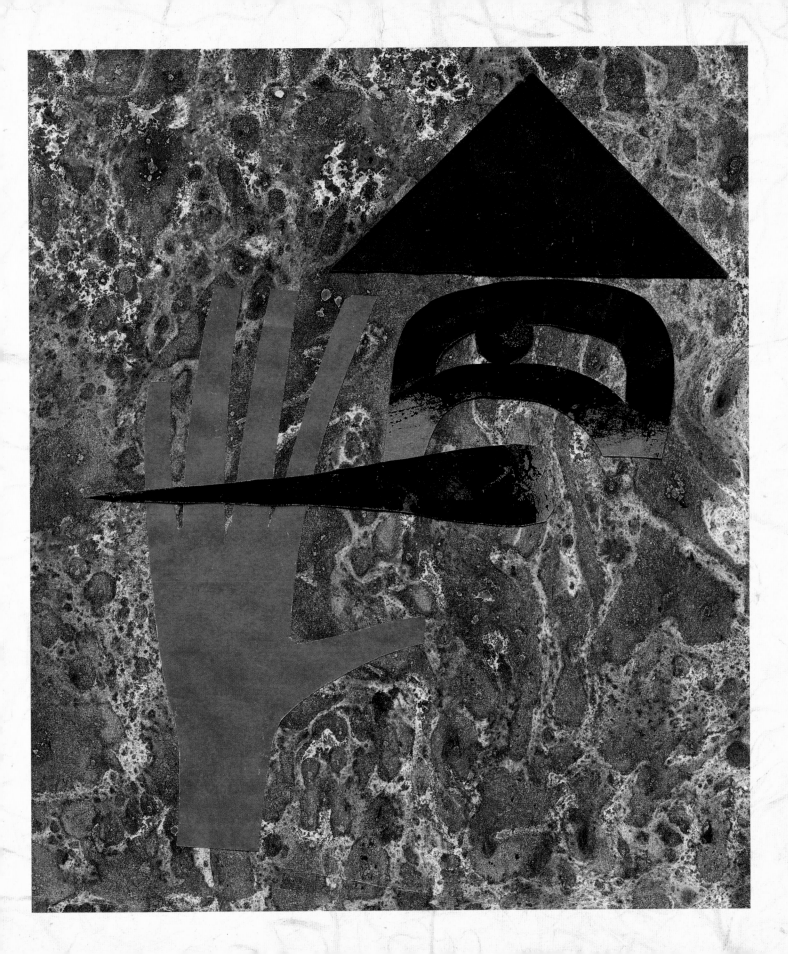

Rudeness

The heart is disrespectful.

 hat

 eyes

 hand

Looking down one's nose is a sign of contempt. Grabbing for something is also an act of rudeness. The heart is rude when it behaves disrespectfully.

Contentment

A peaceful heart.

 claw

work

hand

After a day of hard work, the heart feels peace of mind. It is content.

Despair

An anxious heart.

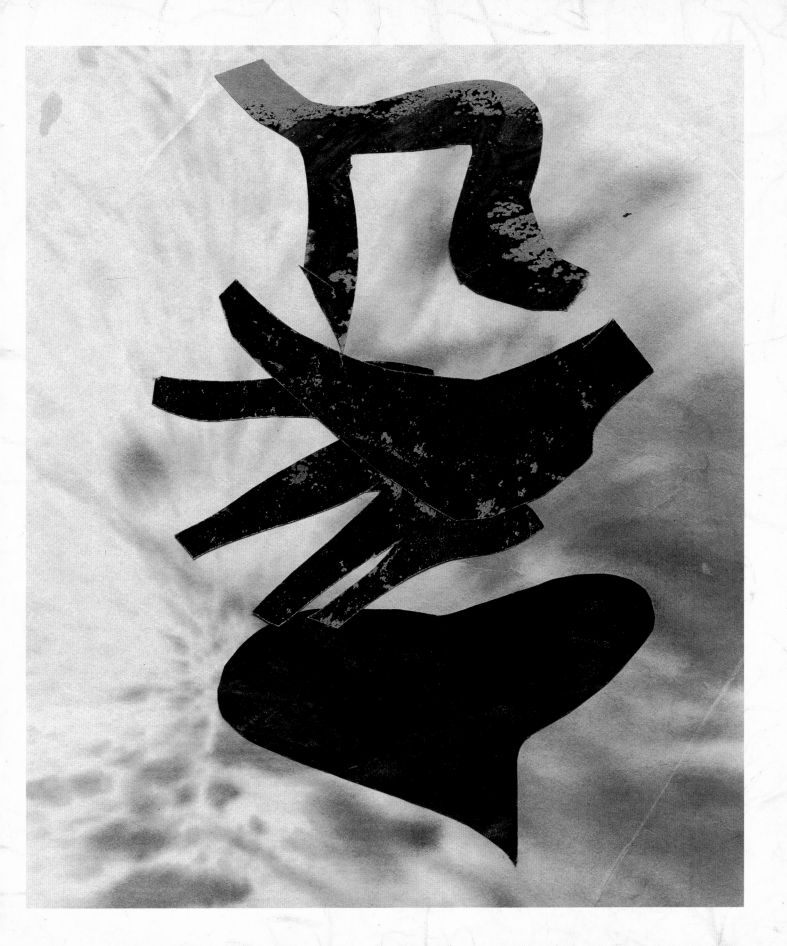

 man

hand

The hand reaches for what it wants. When the heart cannot obtain what it desires, it becomes desperate. It knows despair.

Laziness

An idle heart.

 left hand

 work

 body

 The left hand symbolizes passiveness and inactivity. When eating in Chinese fashion the right hand wields chopsticks, and the left hand holds the rice bowl. As the helping hand, it has the inactive role. When the heart is passive, laziness appears.

Ability

A strong heart.

 head of a bear

 body of a bear

 claws of a bear

A bear can stand upright and use its paws. It has power and capabilities that other animals lack. A person with these characteristics has bearing. When the heart shows generosity and strength of character, it demonstrates ability.

Grace

The heart shows pity.

 confined

 man

 A man who is confined is oppressed. When the heart feels empathy for the oppressed, it has been touched by grace.

Forgetfulness

The heart loses its
sense of purpose.

 man

hides

 This is a man in hiding. When a
man's heart is hidden from him,
he loses sight of it. He becomes
forgetful.

Resentment

The heart is bitter.

 half-moon symbolizing the dark night

curling up

 One who curls up in the dark has given up. When the heart is forced to surrender against its will, this leads to resentment.

Constancy

The heart is faithful.

— heaven and earth

⊖ sun

When the heart is as dependable as the sun in the sky, it understands constancy.

Aspiration

The heart has goals.

 plant

— earth

 When new life appears, just as a budding plant rises from the ground, the heart aspires to new growth and is filled with hope.

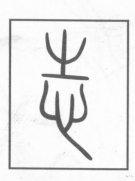

Panic

A frightened heart.

 plants

 hiding

 water

 Plants will not survive without water. When the heart is deprived of what it needs to sustain itself, it experiences panic.

Mercy

A compassionate heart.

Ψ Ψ   delicate plants

8 8   soft and hidden cocoon

ЦΨ   The tender feelings of the
       heart understand compassion.
       This is mercy.

Worry

A fearful heart.

 grain

fire

Centuries ago, in autumn, people prepared for winter by storing crops that could be used as firewood during the difficult times ahead. The heart worries when it has to prepare for difficult times.

Patience

The heart grows tolerant.

 knife

 edge

 When the heart lives on the cutting edge, it calls for care and endurance. This is patience.

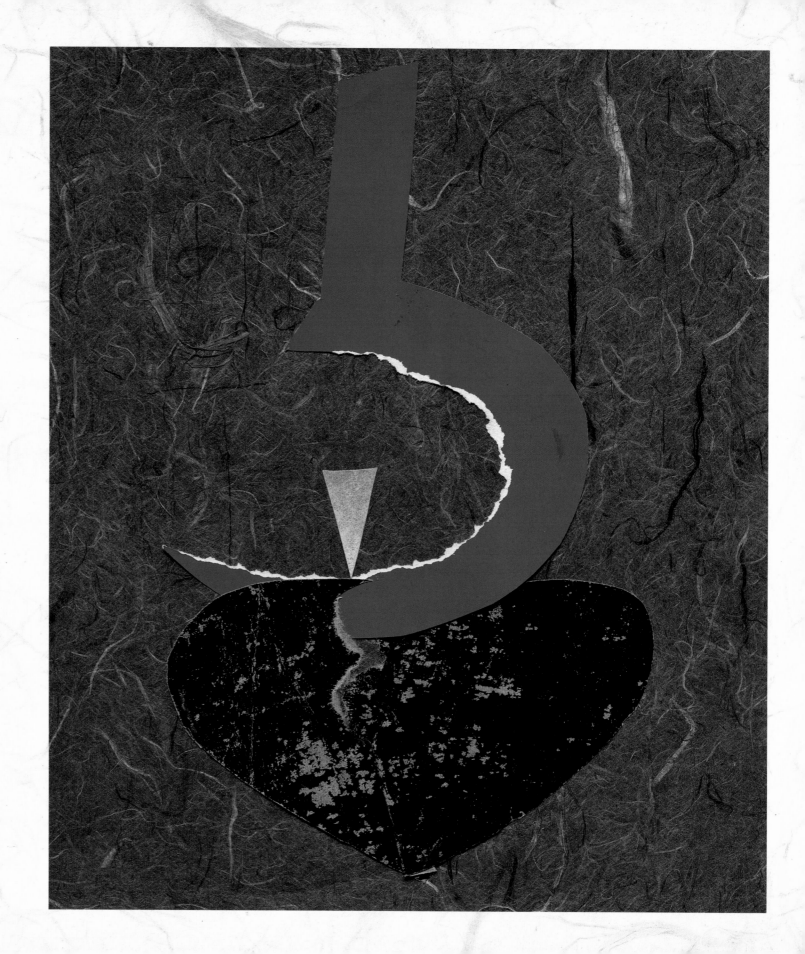

Wrath

An angry heart.

 八　　divided

力　　knife

业　　When the heart is divided,

anger develops.

Stifled

A silenced heart.

 doors

 When the heart is locked
behind doors, it is stifled.

Evil

The heart cannot express its goodness.

 road

 block

 The heart has the potential for goodness, creativity, growth, and the development of one's natural abilities. When the heart is blocked and goodness cannot express itself, evil results.

Doubt

The heart stops trusting.

 weapon

 territory

— land

 Centuries ago, land boundaries were unclear. Warriors couldn't always tell whose territory they were on. Doubt arises when the heart doesn't know where it is.

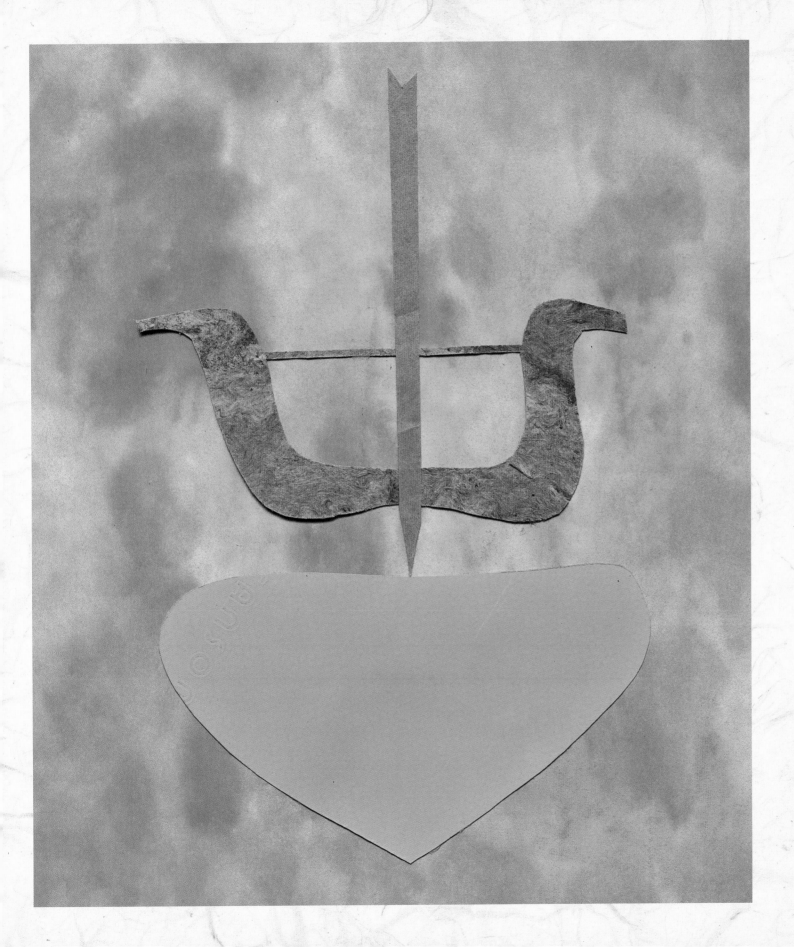

Loyalty

The heart is certain.

 bow

 arrow

 When the heart is centered properly, just as an arrow fits into a bow, it acts with loyalty.

Some years ago, I was taking Tai Chi Chuan classes with Professor M. C. Cheng, known as a master of five excellences: art, calligraphy, poetry, medicine, and Tai Chi Chuan. Tai Chi Chuan is a system of meditation and physical exercises rooted in Chinese cosmology. In one class, during a lecture on Confucius, my teacher's remarks caught my attention. He explained the character 仁, "ren" (often translated as benevolence), which is composed of a respectful man standing to the left of the symbol of heaven and earth. Both symbols are positioned as equals. One who respects another as an equal understands what it is to be benevolent.

仁 also is the homonym for the kernel of a fruit that was used in ancient burials. Professor Cheng told of a true story in which a 4,000-year-old kernel recently unearthed in China sprouted into a tree after receiving moisture and sunshine! I realized that like the kernel, each person has potential which, given the right opportunities and proper nurturing, enables him or her to blossom and flourish. This is benevolence, and it is the basis for creativity, goodness, and the development of one's natural abilities. This manner of studying the ideogram of benevolence kindled in me a renewed interest in interpreting Chinese characters. Certainly these teachings were the basis of the wisdom that had grounded my teacher in his lifetime.

Although the meanings of the Chinese characters are derived from careful research, my main intention was to satisfy my curiosity and reach another level of understanding. Therefore, my interpretation is not so much a work of scholarship but a personal reflection.

In this book, *Voices of the Heart*, I combined visual symbols of the West in the same manner the ancient Chinese used in composing their characters. I focused specifically on characters that contain the heart symbol. The seal style of Chinese calligraphy used is approximately 2,500 years old. It serves as a bridge between the most ancient Chinese pictures and symbols and traditional Chinese characters.

I encourage my readers to use the book as I have, simply as an adventure into a different time and place.   E.Y.